D0512052

Books by Alanna Knight

Fiction

The Legend of the Loch
The October Witch
This Outward Angel
Castle Clodha
Lament for Lost Lovers
The White Rose
A Stranger Came By
The Wicked Wynsleys
The Passionate Kindness (R.L.S. & Fanny Osbourne)
A Drink for the Bridge (Tay Bridge Disaster 1879)
The Black Duchess
Castle of Foxes
Colla's Children

As Margaret Hope

The Queen's Captain
Hostage Most Royal
The Shadow Queen
Perilous Voyage

Plays

The Private Life of Robert Louis Stevenson
(also known as The Passionate Kindness
and Mr. and Mrs. R.L.S.)
Girl on an Empty Swing

Radio Documentaries

Don Roberto: The Life of R.B. Cunninghame Graham
Across the Plains
(Adaptation of R.L. Stevenson's travels in America)

Non Fiction

So You Want to Write
The Robert Louis Stevenson Treasury

SCOTLAND ALIVE SERIES Vol. 2

Edited by Konrad Hopkins and Ronald van Roekel

Cover Design by Craig Maclachlan

THE PRIVATE LIFE OF
ROBERT LOUIS STEVENSON

A One-Act Play

by

Alanna Knight

Adapted for the Stage by John Cairney

't Kan verkeeren.
('Things can change.')

–G.A. Bredero

A RonKon Paperback
WILFION BOOKS, PUBLISHERS
Paisley, Scotland
1984

IBSN 0 905075 17 X

Printed in Great Britain by

PDC Copyprint
65 High Street,
Paisley,
Scotland, U.K.

First published in Great Britain by

Wilfion Books, Publishers
4 Townhead Terrace,
Paisley, Renfrewshire PA1 2AX,
Scotland, U.K.

Now we were to return, like the voyager in the play, and see what rearrangements fortune had perfected the while in our surroundings; what surprises stood ready made for us at home; and whither and how far the world had voyaged in our absence. You may paddle all day long; but it is when you come back at nightfall, and look in at the familiar room, that you find Love or Death awaiting you beside the stove; and the most beautiful adventures are not those we go to seek.

–Robert Louis Stevenson,
An Inland Voyage, 1878

For

Chris and Kevin

CONTENTS

INTRODUCTION
by
Alanna Knight

Robert Louis Stevenson was born in Edinburgh on 13 November 1850, son of Thomas, grandson of Robert Stevenson, of the famous family of lighthouse engineers. A frail child, he spent much of his early life in 17 Heriot Row cared for by his nurse Cummy, his imagination fed on her gory tales from Scottish history. Refusing to follow in the tradition of engineering, he graduated advocate from Edinburgh University, a rebel against everything sacred to his Calvinist upbringing – middle-class morals, the claustrophobic hypocrisy of Victorian society, and organised religion.

With his artist cousin Bob Stevenson, he went to France and there met Mrs. Fanny Osbourne, an American, 'whose eyes are full of sex and mystery', as he described her. Instantly attracted to each other, they fell in love. Their 'long, unglamorous courtship' ended in marriage, a stormy, tortuous but basically fulfilling relationship. There is little doubt that Fanny kept Louis alive.

The curious pair travelled the world searching for a place where Louis might survive, accompanied by an assortment of relatives, servants, and animals. And always, in sickness and in health, Louis wrote: *Treasure Island* begun in Braemar, Scotland, and completed in Davos, Switzerland; *Kidnapped* and *Dr. Jekyll and Mr. Hyde* in Bournemouth, the latter the result of an opium-induced nightmare; *Weir of Hermiston*, incomplete at his death in Samoa, where they settled in 1889. Fanny outlived Louis by twenty years. She died in California in February 1914 and her ashes were taken to Samoa to be buried with her husband.

The Private Life of Robert Louis Stevenson is based on the Stevensons' twenty-year love story. Adapted from my book *The Passionate Kindness*, the play uses first-hand accounts and, wherever possible, the actual words spoken by Louis and Fanny, or from their diaries and letters.

The play takes place in the last hour of Stevenson's life, when in the afternoon of 3 December 1894, he died of a cerebral haemorrhage. Henry James said of the Stevenson marriage that it was 'a fable, strange and romantic as one of Louis's own'.

Aberdeen, Scotland
May 1984

THE PRIVATE LIFE OF
ROBERT LOUIS STEVENSON

A One-Act Play

by

Alanna Knight
Adapted for the Stage by John Cairney

CHARACTERS OF THE PLAY

Louis Stevenson*

Age 44. Tall, thin, dark hair with moustache
Costume: white shirt and trousers, red cummerbund, riding boots
* Pronounced 'Lewis', as in his original full name: Robert Lewis Balfour Stevenson

Fanny Stevenson

Age 55. American. Small, vivacious, grey curly hair
Costume: floor-length smock, bare feet

Cummy

Age indeterminate. Hair under large white cap, spectacles
Costume: Victorian nurse of 1850's

Street Woman

Age indeterminate. Heavily painted, red wig
Costume: red satin dress, feather boa

Note: In the original productions, the three female roles were all played by Miss Rose McBain.

NOTES ON THE SET

Window (Back L); Door (Centre Back) hidden by cane screen; cane chair and sofa (L); desk (R) with chair.

Other properties: books, papers strewn on desk. Photographs in frames. Bright cotton cushions. Potted palms. Native shield and spears, plus rifle decorating wall.

TIME: 3 December 1894. Afternoon

PLACE: The study of Vailima, the Stevensons' home in Samoa

Curtain rises on LOUIS, *writing at desk.*

LOUIS

'Hope, they say, deserts us at no period of our existence. From first to last and in the face of smarting disillusion, we continue to expect good fortune, better health and better conduct; and that so confidently we judge it needless to deserve them. I think it improbable that I shall ever write like Shakespeare, or conduct an army like Hannibal, or distinguish myself like Marcus Aurelius –'

FANNY
(off-stage)

Can't you deal with it, Mother? I'm busy right now.

LOUIS

'And yet I have my by-days, hope prompting, when I am ready to believe I shall go marching down to posterity with divine honours. We have dwelt by choice in a delicious vagueness from our boyhood –'

FANNY *enters.*

FANNY

Seen my work-box anywhere, Louis? Ah, here it is –
(*She takes out sewing.*)

LOUIS
(ignores her, continues)

Listen to this, Fanny. 'Boyhood ceased – well, when? Not I think at twenty, nor perhaps altogether at twenty-five; nor yet at thirty and turned forty, we are still in the thick of that arcadian period. We advance in years somewhat in the manner of an invading army in a barren land; the age we have reached we but hold as an outpost, and still keep open our communications with the extreme rear and first beginnings of the march –'

Well, my dear, and what do you think of that? Fanny?

FANNY *stares out of window.*

LOUIS

Oh dear God, what's the use! A fine one I am to hope.

FANNY *turns.*

FANNY

What's that, dear? Are you all right?

LOUIS

Oh yes, I'm quite all right. For fifteen years I haven't had a day's real health. I've wakened sick and gone to bed weary, but I've done my work unflinchingly in spite of it all. I've written in bed and out of it, written in haemorrhage, in sickness, torn by coughing – written when my head swam from weakness. Oh yes, Fanny – *I'm* all right.

FANNY

But you are better now – (*Resumes sewing.*)

LOUIS

Better? Yes, I'm better now, medically speaking. And have been since we came to Samoa, thank God. (*Moves his shoulder stiffly.*) And yet, there are few days when I'm not in some small distress.

FANNY

Everyone has something, dear. Your mother has her rheumatism and I have my migraines. We are all frail humans, Louis.

LOUIS

That may be so, but I always believed I was made for a contest – not that my battlefield should be the dingy inglorious bed. I would have preferred a place of trumpetings. Fanny! You're not listening.

FANNY

What were you saying, dear?

LOUIS

I was saying that you're not listening. As usual. And you've been back and forward to that window a dozen times today. Tell me, who are you expecting?

FANNY

Expecting? No one —

LOUIS

Fanny — is this another of your little nonsenses?

FANNY

My premonitions haven't always been nonsenses. Quite often they come true.

LOUIS

Your best, as I recall, was that the yacht was going down and we were all to consigned to a watery grave. And what happened? Young Lloyd fell down the ladder and cut his knee.

FANNY

Louis Stevenson — for a man of imagination, I sometimes think you show remarkably little sensitivity.

LOUIS

I know reality from fiction, my dear, if that's what you mean. Fiction is what I write, reality is what I feel.

FANNY

I can't help it — I've been depressed for days now. It's like a dark cloud hovering — as if something is going to happen —

LOUIS

Well, we know it can't be happening to one of us. All the family — yours and mine — are accounted for. All the little lost sheep safely grazing, all in good health and excellent spirits.

FANNY

And eating like horses under this very expensive roof of ours. (*Picks up sheaf of papers from desk.*) Have you looked at this month's crop of bills?

LOUIS

Only briefly — not my favourite reading. Anyway, I'm no longer an excuse for your little dramas. I have developed a tendency to enjoy good health for a change.

FANNY

You'll never know how happy that makes me.

LOUIS

Actually, I haven't felt as fit in donkey's years. I know I grumble about niggling things, but I wish each day was twice as long. I can almost see the years rolling ahead, a strange, serene infinity. On the whole, I feel fine. I've even enjoyed a very persistent homesickness this last week.

FANNY

I thought this was home.

LOUIS

Not for me. Not Samoa — Scotland, always Scotland. And I've had this odd feeling that I'll be seeing it again — very soon —

FANNY

Now, Louis, I hope you're not planning anything in that direction. You know perfectly well what the doctors advised — a return to Scotland would be the death of you.

LOUIS

I'm not planning anything – dammit, woman – why don't you listen to me? It's just a feeling – I wake up every morning as if I'm on the threshold of an exciting journey – turn a corner and there, before my eyes, will be my beloved hills of home.

FANNY

I hope it means that the advance for *Weir of Hermiston* is on its way. Oh, what a help that would be! Our marble halls here at Vailima cost the earth to keep up. Not that you would notice, of course.

LOUIS

You worry about the future far too much, my dear. Live for today, let tomorrow take care of itself. We'll manage, we've always managed – somehow. Fanny, Fanny, quite contrary – how does your garden grow?

FANNY

A lot better, thank you, if you could recognise flowers from weeds –

LOUIS

I only tidied up. Just trying to help –

FANNY

And that enthusiastic half-hour cost me ten dollars for new vegetable seeds. And they were doing so well, the poor little things.

LOUIS *picks up pen.*

LOUIS

Well – off you go and see if any of the new seeds have shown face yet. I promise to keep well away from them.

FANNY

No, I'm not in a gardening mood today. I think I'll go and give the servants a rousting about their inefficiency. That always puts me in a better mood.

LOUIS

You do that, my dear. Scare them into wild activity which, dear God, they do need. Fanny Stevenson, witch woman of the mountains, who has eyes in the back of her head.

FANNY

That's quite unnecessary, Louis. They love me. They're hardly like servants at all, our Vailima family.

LOUIS

Yes, with rather a preponderance of naughty wilful children.

FANNY

I thought your mother would die when she arrived from Edinburgh and found them waiting to greet her in tartan loincloths. She didn't know where to look, poor soul.

LOUIS

Those Royal Stewart loincloths are their livery — makes them members of the Stevenson Clan. They're so proud of them. At least we can sleep safely in our beds without being eaten by our black boys.

FANNY

I suppose cannibalism is really of no consequence, to be politely ignored —

LOUIS

Quite so. Unless it's one of us being eaten.

FANNY

At least you're safe — Tusitala, teller of tales. And God made manifest.

LOUIS
(indicating bills)

Pity his goddess and dependents suffer from such gross appetites. Let's hope that lecture tour in Australia next spring sets us on our feet again. And I'm fit enough now, thank God.

FANNY

Have you written, accepting their invitation?

LOUIS

Just going to, when you can in. (*Seizes pen.*) What's the date?

FANNY

December third.

LOUIS

December – third – 1894. (*Puts down pen.*) Does that date strike you as familiar?

FANNY *shakes her head.*

LOUIS

It must be! An anniversary, isn't it? Something I know well –

FANNY

Didn't we first see Samoa at the beginning of December?

LOUIS

That must be it. Five years ago, almost to the day. A long time for us to be in one place. To be home at last.

FANNY

I must admit that I got rather tired of flying about the world like Noah's dove, with a little olive branch, looking for a place to land —

LOUIS

A place where you could keep me alive — and writing. What a trouble I was to you, my dear. And you didn't care all that much for Samoa either.

FANNY

I never thought we'd settle here. The natives were picturesque — beautiful even — but I didn't like them. They scared me. Especially when I thought our servants would be cannibals. When I wasn't in the kitchen, I dreaded to think what might go into the soup.

LOUIS
(*searching through papers*)

Have you seen that newspaper cutting anywhere?

FANNY

Which one? You get so many these days.

LOUIS

The one Lloyd brought from Apia. Ah, here it is. Listen to this. 'Mr. R.L.S., having proved such an excellent diplomat in the recent Samoan dispute, should be offered a career in politics back in Britain....' —

FANNY

Whoever wrote that was either sarcastic — or crazy.

LOUIS

Perhaps. But I wouldn't change Vailima for any honour - and I must confess, I don't care for politics.

FANNY

That's just because you have too many principles.

LOUIS

Yes, I have. And I'll stick to writing books even if I'm only read by schoolboys, critics and jealous fellow-novelists. My trouble is that I can't mean one thing and write another. 'Sentiment calls for a little gracing' — what moonshine!

FANNY

You're too romantic, that's your problem.

LOUIS

But despite all my romantic notions, I'm also a realist, a most fanatical lover of plain physical sensations, plainly and expressly rendered. I often think that my love of writing is stronger than my love of life itself — that without writing I'd cease to exist.

FANNY

Is this the man who once wrote: 'How can writing compete with life, whose sun we cannot look upon, whose passions waste us —'?

LOUIS

'— and whose desires claim each waking moment. Life infinite in its complications — the beauty of the dawn, the flavour of the wine, the scorching of fire — the bitterness of death.'

FANNY

You make it sound more like the labours of Hercules than the observations of mortal man.

LOUIS

That's it, exactly! Hercules himself, armed with a wee pen and a shilling dictionary.

FANNY

Don't forget the wee tube of pale paint with which to depict the sun's incomparable glory. (*They laugh.*) Life, Louis — and love — you've always had plenty to say on both subjects: 'Love should go out to meet love with open arms' — oh, very neat. What woman of taste could resist such persuasion?

LOUIS

You managed to – for a while.

FANNY

I resisted for three years, let me remind you, before you persuaded me to leave Sam. You were a quite unscrupulous lover.

LOUIS

My dear, I couldn't afford the luxury – or the delay – of long dalliance in our courtship. At Grez we were attended by an air of urgency – and by your family, forever looking over our elbows. Young Lloyd and Belle, not forgetting your husband Sam. Poor Sam, forever about to part form his latest lady-love and appear – decked out in sackcloth and ashes – the prodigal husband returned.

FANNY

You must admit that was a rôle Sam Osbourne played to perfection.

LOUIS

But then he had so much practice.

FANNY

Eighteen years ago – can it really be that long?

LOUIS

1876. The year before my first story was published in *Temple Bar* magazine. And I fondly imagined that event set both my feet firmly planted on the path of writing. At least my travels in France brought forth *An Inland Voyage*.

FANNY

I wonder when you wrote its final words whether they struck you as prophetic?

LOUIS

What was it? Oh yes. 'You may paddle all day long, but it is when you come back at nightfall, and look in at the familiar room, that you find Love or Death awaiting you beside the stove; and the most beautiful adventures are not those we go to seek.' Aye, there was material for another book too –

FANNY

One that will never be written – I hope.

LOUIS

Mrs. Fanny Vandegrift Osbourne, who had entered the art world of Montparnasse with its summer migration to Grez, in the forest of Fontainebleau, to paint, to be quiet and enjoy nature. A respectable married woman – and an *American* – in such company. Incredible!

They move to CENTRE STAGE in spotlight.

FANNY
(in spot)

My husband Sam has gone back home and I can only add, thank goodness. I hate him, but I know that as soon as he beckons, I will weaken and go back to him as I have always done.

LOUIS
(in spot)

The hotel here is excellent, the food and wine, the company – espcially an American, Mrs. Osbourne, whose eyes are full of sex and mystery.

FANNY *steps forward.*

FANNY

Louis Stevenson is male and Scotch and much handsomer than I first thought him.

LOUIS *steps forward.*

LOUIS

Fanny Osbourne is beautiful. I find myself waiting for her appearance each day.

FANNY

He makes a great fuss of me whenever I enter the room, coming at once to my side. He is kindness itself.

LOUIS

The essence of love is kindness. It may best be defined as passionate kindness. Kindness, so to speak, run mad and become importunate.

FANNY

I have never met a man who understood my mind so clearly. It is uncanny. They tell me I am in love, but I am older than he is. He tells me that falling in love is the one illogical adventure, the one thing we are tempted to think of as supernatural in our trite and reasonable world.

LOUIS

Indeed, the ideal story is that of two people who go into love step for step, with a fluttered consciousness, like a pair of children venturing together into a dark room.

FANNY

Two persons, neither of them it may be, very amiable or very beautiful, meet, speak a little, and look a little into each other's eyes –

LOUIS

– That has been done a dozen times or so of times in the experience of either with no great result. But on this occasion, all is different. They fall at once into that state in which another person becomes to us the very gist and centre point of God's creation –

FANNY

– From the first moment when they see each other, with a pang of curiosity, through stage after stage of growing pleasure and embarrassment –

LOUIS

– They can read the expression of their own trouble in each other's eyes. There is here no declaration properly so-called; the feeling is so plainly shared, that as soon as the man knows what is in his own heart, he is sure of what is in the woman's.

They kiss.

Now we were to return, like the voyager in the play, and see what rearrangments fortune had perfected the while in our surroundings; what surprises stood ready made for us at home; and whither and how far the world had voyaged in our absence.

They return to their original positions. Fade spotlight.

FANNY

And what did we discover, Louis?

LOUIS

That marriage is like life that it is a field of battle and not a bed of roses. Marriage is one long conversation, chequered by disputes, but in the intervals, the whole material of life is turned over and, in process of time, without sound of trumpet, they conduct each other into new worlds of thought –

FANNY

But we are happy now – aren't we?

LOUIS

Your tone implies some doubt about it.

FANNY

We quarrel —

LOUIS

We also love. So we have the best of both worlds, the heights and the depths. We live, Fanny — we live — and that is the most important of all.

FANNY

Whoever would believe, to look at us now, a respectable middle-aged couple, that our illicit love was once the scandal of Paris?

LOUIS

And it rocked the drawing rooms of Edinburgh too!

FANNY

For you to take on such odds, with your Calvinist Heriot Row background.

LOUIS

My parents were shocked — scandalised. The poor good people. That's the trouble with respectable folk, they are so rarely cheerful. And if your morals make you dreary, you can depend on it — they are wrong.

FANNY

It wasn't very pleasant for me, remember. Knowing I loved you, trying to make my marriage work for the sake of the children, despite Sam's eternal philanderings. Sam — whom I could neither live with nor without. But I never expected you to follow me to California and persuade me into that divorce.

LOUIS

And small thanks, as I remember, did I get when I arrived on your doorstep.

FANNY

What did you expect? Looking like a scarecrow, more dead than alive with fever — dysentery. That terrible journey across half the world. You must have been mad.

LOUIS

Mad with love —

FANNY

We were the scandal of Monterey, that American woman who lives openly with her literary lover — and both of them visited regularly by her legal husband.

LOUIS

Our sleeping arrangements must have intrigued them.

FANNY

I expected a lover, Louis. Not an invalid, with me to watch over him at the gates of death, always sure he'd slip through them the moment my back was turned. I was more nurse than mistress.

LOUIS

A long, unglamorous courtship that would have daunted most couples, we had. Fraught with illness, poverty — yet you managed with the passing years to turn it into a romance of destiny, a charming operetta, which you have persuaded all our friends — and ourselves — to believe in.

FANNY

It hasn't been lacking in moments of drama. Once I recall, when the fever was on you, you sat up in bed and sang — sang, damn you — in the middle of the night, in a large, croaking, horrible voice, just like a madman. Another time, I thought you were dead, drowned in blood, unable to speak. They you took up a pencil and wrote in a steady hand: 'Don't worry, if this is death, then it is an easy one.'

LOUIS

Worse than death, I could see the spectre of disinheritance looming over the water in Heriot Row. A charming operetta indeed!

FANNY

But what a honeymoon we had —

LOUIS

One I shall never forget — with your young Lloyd — and our usual menagerie of domestic beasts.

FANNY

Not a care in the world though. Full of confidence for the future — we must have been crazy.

LOUIS

Not many lovers would choose a derelict mining camp at Silverado.

FANNY

And what a wedding night!

LOUIS

I took cramp and you smashed your thumb mending the leaky roof of the only habitable shack.

FANNY

I still have the scar.

LOUIS

And then you and Lloyd took diphtheria and I had to hustle you back down the mountain to civilisation and the only doctor.

FANNY

In an open cart — we must have looked like refugees from the plague. I often wonder what would have become of us, if your parents hadn't relented and sent the boat fare to Liverpool.

LOUIS

What a welcome they gave us – not untinged, I fancy, with gratitude that the American divorcee who was their new daughter-in-law, wasn't a pistol-packin' pioneer or a flamboyant harpy.

FANNY

You must admit that the Bohemian cigarette–smoking lady in her black silk stockings – and her literary lover always behaved with the utmost decorum and good taste –

LOUIS

Always – always – until the door was safely closed.

FANNY

Your mother was at great pains to inform me the very first day I followed her upstairs in Heriot Row, that she had breathed a sigh of relief, ye ken, when she saw I was so ordinary. Not very flattering, was it? But comforting in the circumstances.

LOUIS

Especially when she confided to me: 'We kenned the meenit we saw yer leddy wife, that she was a sensible wee soul.'

FANNY

She hinted to me – more than once – that my obvious good taste in taking you as husband might reasonable extend to acting as brake on your wayward behaviour, eccentric habits and weird attire. I overheard her telling your old nurse Cummy that I was 'mebbe not quite the daughter-in-law she had imagined'.

LOUIS

But a guid wee soul. Always that. And so you were, and are. How extraordinary it was to be home again in that house. What floods of old memories –

FANNY

And not the only floods we had to contend with — That weather you had warned me about —

LOUIS

In Edinburgh, my dear, the delicate die early — and I have sometimes been tempted to envy them. Edinburgh weather — raw, boisterous in winter, shifty and uncongenial in summer — and a downright meteorological purgatory in spring. The vilest climate under heaven, beaten upon by all the winds that blow, drenched with rain, buried in cold sea fogs, and powdered with snow as it comes flying across the Highlands. Edinburgh Castle — there's a sight! A Bass Rock on dry land, rooted in a garden shaken by passing trains and casting its warlike shadow over a valley set with trees —

FANNY

While from their smoky beehives ten storeys high along the Royal Mile, the great unwashed look down upon open squares and the gardens of the wealthy, sunning themselves along Princes Street with its splendid commercial palaces. Er — have you seen my scissors?

LOUIS

Scissors? No, I haven't. Ah — Edinburgh —

FANNY

Edinburgh — and you with pleurisy, then bronchitis. When you started spitting blood, I lost my rôle as nurse, and old Cummy moved in with her home-made remedies, her old wives' tales. And her determination that wife or no wife, there was no other body in the world but herself who knew what was best for her laddie. (*Searches in work-box.*) Now, where are those damned scissors? Nobody in this family has the slightest respect for other people's property.

Exit. **FANNY. LOUIS** *takes up photograph.*

LOUIS

Ah, dear Cummy. She was more patient with me than an angel. Sometimes she would lift me out of bed and take me, rolled in blankets, to the window, so that I might look into the blue night starred with street lamps, and see where the gaslight still burned in other sickrooms; and other little boys would be watching with their nurses for the morning.

Kisses photograph and opens book:

> 'For the long nights you lay awake
> And watched for my unworthy sake;
> For your most comfortable hand
> That led me through the uneven land;
> For all the story-books you read;
> For all the pains you comforted;
> For all you pitied, all you bore,
> In sad and happy days of yore –
> My second Mother, my first Wife,
> The angel of my infant life – '

STAGE darkens. **CUMMY** *enters, carrying candle. Walks to sofa, smooths cushions.*

CUMMY

> 'When I was sick and lay a-bed,
> I had two pillows at my head,
> And all my toys beside me lay,
> To keep me happy all the day.'

LOUIS
(in childish voice)

> 'And sometimes for an hour or so
> I watched my leaden soldiers go,
> With different uniforms and drill,
> Among the bedclothes, through the hills.'

CUMMY

'And sometimes sent my ships in fleets
All up and down the sheets;
Or brought my trees and houses out,
And planted cities all about.'

LOUIS

(as before)

'I was the giant great and still
That sits upon the pillow-hill,
And sees before him dale and plain,
The pleasant land of counterpane.'

CUMMY

'It is very nice to think
The world is full of meat and drink,
With little children saying grace
In every Christian kind of place.'

LOUIS

(as before)

'When I am grown to man's estate
I shall be very proud and great,
And tell the other girls and boys
Not to meddle with my toys.'

CUMMY

'Whenever the moon and stars are set,
Whenever the wind is high;
All night long in the dark and wet,
A man goes riding by.
Late in the night when the fires are out,
Why does he gallop and gallop about?
Whenever the trees are crying aloud,
And ships are tossed at sea,
By, on the highway, low and loud,
By at the gallop goes he.
By at the gallop goes he, and then
By he comes back at the gallop again!

CUMMY *laughs. Blows out candle. Exits.*

STAGE in darkness. LIGHTS go up on **LOUIS**, *slumped over desk. Raises head, staggers from desk towards window. SOUND of storm, lightning flash.*

FANNY
(off-stage)

Yes, I know it's raining, Mother. Yes, I'll ask Louis if he wants his tea now.

FANNY *enters.*

FANNY

Well, you wanted Scotland, Louis. How's this weather as a cure for homesickness?

LOUIS *remains motionless at window. She goes to him, touches his shoulder. He springs away from her.*

FANNY

Louis, what the devil is wrong with you?

LOUIS

Oh, it's only you. Dear God, for a moment I thought you were Cummy. (*Laughs uneasily.*)

FANNY

Cummy?

LOUIS

Yes. (*Shakes head, bewildered.*) I must have nodded off for a moment. Thought she came in here – walked about. A strange vivid dream I had.

FANNY

It's all this talk about the past. Your mother is at it as well – reminding me how we all fled from Edinburgh that first summer.

LOUIS

My fault again. I imagined a pleasant Highland holiday would be the answer. In Pitlochry –

FANNY

Where it rained – and rained.

LOUIS

We fled to Braemar, where it blew a great deal and rained in proportion. We had to pass a good deal of time between four walls in that house lugubriously known as 'the late Miss McGregor's cottage'. Cold – and damp. What a summer.

FANNY

The Queen didn't mind the weather, she seemed to thrive on it.

LOUIS

I ken well how she drove past each day from Balmoral, staring straight ahead, oblivious of the rain in her open carriage.

FANNY

Armed with good intentions and a tea basket – a tea basket, I ask you, for an open-air picnic.

LOUIS

Those two ladies-in-waiting, stiff with cold, their complexions mauve.

FANNY

And don't forget John Brown – beautiful John Brown.

LOUIS

He was known to eye the atrocious weather and remark to his Royal mistress: 'Aye, ma'am, it's pleasantly cool, ye ken, pleasantly cool the day.'

FANNY

At least Braemar was a case of good coming from bad. If it hadn't been for my Lloyd, bored out of his mind, drawing that map, your *Treasure Island* would never have been conceived.

LOUIS

I can still see that map – the extraordinary way in which the characters began to appear. Next thing, I was writing out a list of chapters.

FANNY

A story for boys, you called it. No need for psychology or fine writing, you said.

LOUIS

And I had a boy at hand to act as a touchstone.

FANNY

I wasn't surprised when it did well as a boy's serial, but for Cassell to want to publish it – wasn't that wonderful?

LOUIS

Especially when they offered a hundred, jingling, tingling, golden-minted quid for the privilege. Dear God, how we needed the money. It was dreadful to be a great big man with a family – and not be able to buy bread.

FANNY

You were lucky to be alive, let alone buying bread.

LOUIS

Alive? Is that what you call it? Fleeing like migrant birds across Europe, searching for some sunny shore which might work a miracle of restored health.

FANNY

Davos is one place I shall never forget. That awful bleak world of snow and mountains – a black and white sterile wilderness.

LOUIS

Yes, even the shopkeepers were consumptive.

FANNY

France was a considerable improvement. Remember Campagne Defli?

LOUIS

Debug or Demosquito would have been equally appropriate names.

FANNY

I loved its aromatic garden, but it didn't compare with our little doll's house at Hyères. Until your tribe of hard-drinking friends descended on us.

LOUIS

A mere fleeting visit, en route to Nice.

FANNY

That had me racing after you to gather up the pieces at the end of your great carouse. The British doctor scared me out of my wits with his suggestion that some man friend be summoned, to take care of your funeral arrangements.

LOUIS

Ah, there I was, shorn of my grog for ever. A kidney infection, of all things. My last pleasure gone. I was myself no more. Of that feverish, voluble, whiskified zany Scot who once sparked through Europe, bent on art and the pleasures of the flesh, naught would remain but the strong language. That at least, I shall take gravewards. My last word shall be an execration.

FANNY

There were plenty of those at Hyères. But I did love our Chalêt la Solitude. I even thought for a while I was pregnant.

LOUIS

Hyères — the only place where I was truly happy. That garden — I would swear that angels frequented it.

FANNY

Your magic garden, alas, was fed by a cesspool. Typhus soon had us on the march again.

LOUIS

Bournemouth did seem a splendid idea. That nest of retired Army colonels and old sea-dogs. Besides a climate guaranteed for geriatrics, couldn't be all that bad for me.

FANNY

Lloyd was so thrilled, near enough to boarding school for him to come home to tea. He missed you more than anyone. You were always more his elder brother than his stepfather.

LOUIS

And didn't that upset the neighbours. 'D'ye allow the lad to call you Louis? 'Tain't decent — disrespectful, that's what. Should be calling you Papa.' When I pointed out that I had not that honour, our colonel sniffed and said: 'Have him call you Sir then.'

FANNY

You were very popular in our lovely Skerryvore – despite the neighbours. And I learned – fast – that I was only wife to the famous Mr. R.L.S. Most of the callers thought I was the servant, opening the door, keeping them at bay when you were ill and on opium to make you sleep.

LOUIS

What dreams it brought! Not for the faint-hearted, I can tell you.

FANNY

You wakened me screaming one night. There you lay, eyes wide open, pointing a finger at your clenched fist, crawling across the bedclothes. Horrible it was.

LOUIS

If you'd left me alone, I would have had the finest of all bogey tales. I wonder how many other writers have had the extreme good fortune to be presented with the entire plot of a novel in a dream?

FANNY

It was very nearly your last novel. Ill as you were – writing, writing –

LOUIS

And ten weeks later it was published. A sensation! Subject of a sermon in St. Paul's – and lesser pulpits up and down the country. We gave the English language a new phrase –

FANNY

How you enjoyed signing letters : 'I hope, Jekyll, I fear, Hyde'.

LOUIS

I fear if my father had not died in Edinburgh, we might never have left Bournemouth. We'd still be there.

FANNY

You wouldn't, Louis. You would be dead. It's Samoa that has kept you alive.

LOUIS

And yet my sense of home – of Scotland, remains so strong.

FANNY

Well, I seldom think of California these days. There's nothing for me there and I don't suppose I'll ever see San Francisco again.

LOUIS

How I envy you that complete uprooting. Even standing on the verandah of an evening, I can feel Scotland. The scent of peat smoke, the rush of brown swirling water, the sting of clear air – aye, and the taste of good Scotch whisky. Oh, the indescribable bite of the whole thing: 'Be it granted me to behold you again in dying, Hills of Home.'

FANNY

Come now, Louis, no need to be morbid – you've plenty to be grateful for.

LOUIS

I do wish I'd been – kinder – to my parents.

FANNY

You're the apple of your mother's eye – always have been. She thinks the sun rises and sets with you each day. And she never lets any one of us forget it.

LOUIS

Oh, I don't mean now – I mean in those Heriot Row days when I was young. What a curse I was to my poor parents.

FANNY

To hear your mother tell it, no one would ever believe that you were a real bad boy, Louis Stevenson. Frequenting howffs in Leith Walk, going home drunk, toying with atheism, flouting your middle-class conventions – and worse. (*Picks up picture and pretends to dust it.*) Swanston Cottage. Such a pretty place for romantic dalliance. Kate Drummond – wasn't that her name.?

LOUIS
(*sharply*)

What do you know about Kate Drummond?

FANNY
(*sweetly*)

Nothing. Only that she was a woman of the streets.

LOUIS

The exact term is an Edinburgh whore.

FANNY

You don't need to be exact – I've read *Claire*.

LOUIS

Which you have every intention of destroying when I am gone.

FANNY

That is quite uncalled for, Louis. *Claire* is a bad book which would not enhance your reputation in the slightest –

LOUIS

My reputation – which you consider your duty to protect for posterity. Is that it?

FANNY

I have to protect you from yourself, Louis. People –

LOUIS

To hell with people —

FANNY

There is no need to be coarse. You have always relied on my judgement. You know I'm right and one day you'll be glad I advised you against sending *Claire* to the publishers. What would the literary world think of such a sordid story?

LOUIS

Even an autobiographical one?

FANNY

How could you even entertain such a thought? After all I've done for you, the sacrifices I've made. Kate Drummond — or Claire as you so thinly disguise her — her existence in your life is an affront to me —

LOUIS

Not again, Fanny — please — not again.

FANNY

Your friends think little enough of me as it is. They hate me, all of them. How they would snigger and whisper and shake their heads —

LOUIS

Don't be any idiot, Fanny. The only reason why my friends — if any of them knowing you, could ever think little of you, is because they see you taking me over, body and soul. Even to choosing who shall be my friends and what I shall write.

FANNY

Friends — are they what you call friends? I have a better name —

LOUIS

For God's sake, Fanny, let's have an end to it. An end — do you hear? Let's not bruise our souls by tearing that old meat apart — again — for pity's sake —

FANNY

Louis Stevenson –

LOUIS

Leave me alone!

FANNY

By God – you would try the patience of an angel.

Exit **FANNY.**

LOUIS

An angel, eh? 'To marry is to domesticate the recording angel' – I was wise when I wrote that. 'Times are changed with him who marries, the road lies long and straight and dusty to the grave. Once you are married, there is nothing left for you – not even suicide – but to be good.'

Takes up picture.

Kate, oh Kate, I wonder where the tide of life and love abandoned you–

'She came, she went. In other lands,
Perchance in fairer skies,
Her hands shall cling with other hands,
Her eyes to other eyes.
She vanished. In the sounding town,
Will she remember too?
Will she recall the eyes of brown
As I recall the blue?'

STAGE darkens briefly. **WOMAN** *appears in spot.*

WOMAN

Weel now, if that isna' Velvet Coat. Hoo's ma laddie the nicht? Aye, aye, ye're lookin' braw. C'mon, Velvet Coat, y'gonna be nice to me the nicht agen, y'gonna buy me a wee drink — Ah've a helluva thirst.

LOUIS *comes into spot, stares past her.*

LOUIS

Who's she?

WOMAN

Who? Where?

LOUIS

That girl — by the door.

WOMAN

Oh *that* — she's Kate.

LOUIS

Kate —

WOMAN

From the Highlands — thinks a lot o' hersel'.

LOUIS

She's beautiful.

WOMAN

New to the game — came to us last week. Only a bit bairn, like yersel'. Seventeen, she is. What a waste in a place like the Gay Japanee. Ye'd ha' thocht she'd fetch a better price in them posh howffs, ower where ye bide. She'll no stay bonny lang on Leith Walk, Ah can tell ye. Sez she has principles. She'll no dance, nor tak off her claes — weel, no in public, that is. Principles is askin' for trouble — an' bein' out of a job. Ah hear there's no complaints from the fellas tho' — Ye havena' heard a bloody word Ah've said. Awa' tae hell wi' ye. Half-a-lassie, half-a-laddie, half a yella' yite — that's what they ca' ye in Queen Street. If ye fancy her a' that, why d'ye no' marry her, Velvet Coat — d'ye think ye could manage it, if ye did, eh?

LOUIS

Marry Kate Drummond. Marry a woman of the streets. My poor father. He wished he had never survived, never lived to see the day when his son added whoring to atheism. 'I have made all my life to suit you, my only child. I have worked for you, gone out of my way for you and I would ten times sooner see you lying in your grave than that you would be shaking the faith of other young men and bringing ruin on other houses, as you have on mine. As for your poor mother, this is the heaviest affliction that has ever befallen her.'

What a damned curse I was to my parents. The love of parents for their children is, of all natural affections, the most ill-starred. It is not love for the person, since it begins before that person has come into the world and founds upon an imaginary character and looks. They have been like the duck and hatched swan's eggs or the other way round; yet they tell themselves with miserable penitence that the blame lies with them, and had they laid more closely, the swan would have been a duck — and homekeeping, in spite of it all.

Enter **FANNY**. *She puts her arms around him.*

FANNY

Mother was just reminding me, for the second time today, how she sold a good home and gave up everything to make her home here with us at Vailima. And having survived the Arctic conditions at Saranac Lake that first winter, she never thought she'd have to contend with housekeeping on a series of assorted craft in the South Seas. At least she was never sea-sick.

LOUIS

Too busy converting heathen sailors. How they used to take to their heels when they saw her approaching, Bible in hand.

FANNY

As for poor Captain Otis, what a shock we were to him. And he thought your *Treasure Island* needed lessons in seamanship and said so. Your mother was black affronted, especially when he turned down a signed copy of *Jekyll and Hyde.*

LOUIS

'No, ma'am, thank you, ma'am. Having read one of his books, I see no good reason to try another.' (*They laugh.*)

FANNY

I shall never forget the sight of your mother in her widow's cap and streamers, the very spit of Queen Victoria above the neck, with a body fetchingly attired in the *holuku.* (*Touches her gown.*) The most comfortable garments the missionaries could have imagined, to cover a woman's nakedness. Oh Louis, we've done such mad things, haven't we?

LOUIS

I seem to remember an added complication on the voyage.

FANNY

Oh yes, I thought I was pregnant again. After all those years. And me, a grandmother.

LOUIS

I'd been through it all before when our enchanted world at Hyères seemed likely to be invaded by the patter of small feet. Let's face it, my darling girl. We were both a little too antique – if our marriage had seemed ludicrous to some – what would we look like pushing a tiny baby in a perambulator and forever being mistaken for its grandparents. And yet, I was just getting used to the idea and, I may say, feeling very proud of myself –

FANNY

When it came to naught, I cried for days.

LOUIS

So did I. Our baby would have been no ordinary child, of that I'm sure. But we had plenty of other adventures if that of parenthood was denied us.

FANNY

Storms and perils on sea, Christianised cannibals on land.

LOUIS

Whom I suspected still kept cold missionary on the sideboard.

FANNY

Remember King Tembinok —

LOUIS

The Napoleon of the Gilberts. Notorious for boarding trading vessels and buying whatever took his fancy. Only a very brave man would have refused his smiling offer, however inadequate.

FANNY

His thatched palace was packed with rusting weapons, broken clocks and his wardrobe — frockcoat worn with lady's bloomers, sunbonnet crowned by top hat. No one laughed — no one dared —

LOUIS

Besides, he did wear them with certain aplomb.

FANNY

And when he heard that Mr. Stevenson was one of Queen Victoria's subjects, he thought we had Royal connections. Nothing was too good for us after that.

LOUIS

Breadfruit instead of bullets. What a man, he even shed tears when we sailed away. But Samoa lay ahead, just a speck on the distant horizon. We didn't know it then, but the voyage was almost over. We had sailed into harbour at last.

FANNY

Odd, wasn't it? As if it had been lying in wait.

LOUIS

I'm glad we came and settled down. But I'm still wistful for Edinburgh winds and there are nights when I'd sell my soul to stand on Waverley Bridge and watch the trains go by, as I did so long ago. Did I say I'd sell my soul? Well, that would be about the price demanded.

FANNY

Don't you ever forget it. Keep on playing Highland chieftain, even if Samoa is no glen – and this Vailima of ours is a monster, to be fed on millions of words which you must write.

LOUIS

Everyone lives by selling something. But yours is the energy that keeps the pot boiling. You doctor everyone and cannot be doctored yourself. Poor Fanny, you dream dreams and see visions.

FANNY

But you're the one who's subject to trances. The tame celebrity. You smoke too much, except when coughing – or kissing. (*They kiss and he coughs apologetically.*) You're hopelessly entangled in apron-strings – and you drink too much. As for your language, it's shocking and your temper is quite unstable.

LOUIS

I'm also addicted to explaining the universe. Scotch, ma'am, Scotch. (*Hands her paper.*) Go on, read it.

FANNY
(*reading*)

'To My Wife
'I saw rain falling and the rainbow drawn
On Lammermuir. Hearkening I heard again
In my precipitous city beaten bells. And here afar,

•Intent on my own race and place, I wrote.
  'Take thou the writing: Thine it is. For who
Burnished the sword, blew on the drowsy coal,
Held still the target higher, chary of praise
And prodigal of counsel — who but thou?
So now, in the end, if this the least be good,
If any deed be done, if any fire
Burn in the imperfect page, the praise be thine.'

Oh Louis, it's beautiful — beautiful —

LOUIS

It's the dedication of *Weir of Hermiston* — if I ever get it finished —

FANNY

What's wrong, darling? You're shivering.

LOUIS

I felt odd there, for a moment. Geese on my grave —

FANNY

Catch one for the pot then. The kitchen calls and the pantry is empty. A nice fat goose would be splendid.

LOUIS

Don't joke, Fanny. Wait a moment —

FANNY

Yes?

LOUIS

Do you remember where the road crosses the burn under Glencorse Church?

FANNY

We had a picnic there once with your parents – a lovely spot.

LOUIS

When I'm gone, go there and say a prayer for me. Shut your eyes, and see if I don't appear to you. Oh yes – and let it be a Sunday –

FANNY

You're getting as morbid as old Cummy. You need cheering up, my lad.

LOUIS

I often think I owe what I am today to Cummy.

FANNY

And don't I know that – and so does the entire world.

SOUND of ship's hooter.

That'll be the mailboat. I'll just send one of the boys down. Pray for a cheque this time –

LOUIS

Wait – light the lamp before you go. It's getting dark –

FANNY

Nonsense, dear. It's only five o'clock and your tea is nearly ready.

Exit **FANNY.**

STAGE darkens

LOUIS
(as if repeating incantation)

'My tea is nearly ready and the sun has left the sky,
It's time to take the window to see Leerie going by;
For every night at tea-time and before you take your seat,
With lantern and with ladder he comes posting up the street – '

Edinburgh? Where are you, damn you? Can't see you but I know
you're lurking about somewhere out there. Appear, blast you!
'For we are very lucky with a lamp before the door –'
Cummy? Is that you, Cummy?
'Whenever the moon and stars are set –'
The storm – the storm – Cummy!
'By at the gallop goes he –
By he comes back at the gallop again –'
Oh, Cummy, Cummy – the storm – it's so noisy. And my head
hurts –

CUMMY *enters.*

CUMMY

It's the Good Lord that comes in a roarin' storm and snatches up
wicked bairns frae their cosy warm beds and hurls them doon to the
black pit wi' the Devil. Guid wee bairns hae naethin' to fear. There, there,
ma laddie, sleep the noo.

LOUIS

Cummy – Cummy – I'm sick – I'm awfa' sick. Give me your hand,
Cummy – it's getting dark.

CUMMY *takes his hand, leads him to sofa.*

CUMMY

'For we are very lucky, with a lamp before the door,
And Leerie stops to light it as he lights so many more;
And O! before you hurry by, with ladder and with light,
O Leerie, see a little child and nod to him tonight.'

LOUIS

Dark – dark – stop it getting dark, Cummy.

CUMMY

There, there, bairnie. It's just a bad dream ye're havin'. It'll be far awa'
come morn. Sleep the noo, and if ye're a guid wee laddie, Cummy'll tak
ye to see a' they braw angels at Greyfriars Kirkyard –

LOUIS

Oh God, my head – what a pain. Do I look strange? (*Falls back.*)

CUMMY *bends over him.*

CUMMY

There's ma guid wee mannie. (*Closes his eyes.*) Ye're safe wi' Cummy.
A grand long sleep and ye'll be ready for Cummy to tak ye to the kirkyard
- if it disna' rain.

STAGE darkens.

FANNY
(*off-stage*)

Louis – Louis – *LOUIS!*

SOUND of her footsteps. **FANNY** *enters.*

Louis – oh dear God – *No!*

LOUIS
(voice only)

'Under the wide and starry sky
Dig the grave and let me lie,
Glad did I live and gladly die,
  And I laid me down with a will.
'This be the verse you grave for me:
Home he lies where he longed to be,
Home is the sailor, home from sea,
  And the hunter, home from the hill.'

SOUND of native drums.

SILENCE.

CURTAIN

SCOTLAND ALIVE SERIES

Vol. 1. *The Common Bond* by John Rodgers
ISBN 0 905075 11 0   ii + 107pp., 1980
A RonKon Paperback: £2.00 U.K./$5.00 U.S.A. and Canada

A historical and biographical study of some of the common ties
between Scotland and North America.

Vol. 2. *The Private Life of Robert Louis Stevenson*
A One-Act Play by Alanna Knight. Adapted for the Stage by John
Cairney
ISBN 0 905075 17 X   **v +   40** pp., 1984
A RonKon Paperback: £2.95 U.K./$6.00 U.S.A./ Canada/ Australia

The highly acclaimed play based on the love story of one of
Scotland's favourite authors and his American wife.

Vol. 3. *The Wilsons: Their Origins and Past* by John G. Wilson.
Illustrated, and with Maps
ISBN 0 905075 18 8   56pp., 1984
A RonKon Paperback: £3.00 U.K./ £3.25 rest of the world

A detailed examination of the genealogy of the Wilson family in
Great Britain, with special attention to Scotland and Northern
Ireland, and references to the U.S.A.

WILFION BOOKS, PUBLISHERS
4 Townhead Terrace
Paisley, Renfrewshire PA1 2AX
Scotland, U.K.

Notes